QUIZ
FA

PEOPLE
& PLACES

Kingfisher Books, Grisewood & Dempsey Ltd,
Elsley House, 24–30 Great Titchfield Street, London W1P 7AD

First published in 1993 by Kingfisher Books
10 9 8 7 6 5 4 3 2 1

Some of the material in this edition was previously published by Kingfisher Books in
Question & Answer Encyclopedia: _Why Is It?, What Is It?, Where Is It?,_
When Did It Happen?, Who Were They?

British Library Cataloguing-in-Publication Data
A catalogue record for this book is available from the British Library

ISBN 0 86272 993 9

Edited by Cynthia O'Neill
Designed and typeset by Talkback International Limited
Printed by BPCC Hazells, Aylesbury, Buckinghamshire

QUIZ
FACTS
PEOPLE
& PLACES

Quiz Questions by
Janice Lacock
with Annabel Else

Kingfisher Books

WHY DO BALLERINAS WEAR BLOCKED SHOES?

Blocked shoes, with square solid toes, are used by ballerinas who dance on the tips of their toes, a position known as on pointe*. The peculiar shape of these shoes makes it easier for them to balance.*

It takes considerable skill for a ballerina to do pointe work. Girls usually have at least two years of experience before they begin. The first exercises are performed with the help of the barre. Later the dancers train in the centre of the studio floor. Traditionally, only ballerinas dance on *pointe*. Male dancers do not perform this movement.

QUIZ 1

1 *What is the sailor's hornpipe?*
2 *What dancer was strangled by her own scarf?*
3 *Where would you find flamenco dancing?*
4 *What sort of dancers wear tutus?*
5 *Who wrote the music to* Swan Lake*?*
6 *Which ballet is set at Christmas?*
7 *Who was Ginger Rogers's famous dancing partner?*
8 *Who devises the steps of a dance?*
9 *How many people dance a* pas de deux*?*
10 *What ballet is about Princess Aurora?*

WHO WAS ANNA PAVLOVA?

Anna Pavlova (1882–1931) was a great Russian ballerina who was famous for her solo performances, especially one called **The Dying Swan.**

She became internationally famous in 1909, when she travelled with a company made up of dancers from the Mariinsky and Bolshoi theatres – the *Ballets Russes*. In 1913, Pavlova set up her own company with her husband.

WHEN DID MODERN DANCE APPEAR?

Modern dance developed at the beginning of the 20th century. There were two styles – one in Europe and one in America.

European modern dance explored ideas about the body in relation to space. American modern dance drew inspiration from other cultures. New ballets were based on ancient ritual and myth, as well as modern subjects. The themes were the heart of their dances, instead of being just an aid to the techniques of movement.

WHO WAS VASLAV NIJINSKY?

Vaslav Nijinsky (1890-1950) was one of the greatest-ever male ballet dancers – known for his amazingly high leaps (elevation) and his extremely expressive and dramatic interpretations. He was also a great choreographer, producing controversial new ballets.

He was a star even before he had finished training. When he joined the Mariinsky Theatre, he partnered some of the greatest ballerinas of the day. He was a resounding success in Paris with the *Ballets Russes*.

He left the stage in 1919 after a nervous breakdown.

QUIZ 2

1 Which female singing voice can reach the highest note?

2 Which male singing voice can reach the lowest note?

3 What type of singing voice does Pavarotti have?

4 What does a barbershop quartet do?

5 What instruments are used to accompany a barbershop quartet?

6 What is a euphonium?

7 What instrument did Adolphe Sax invent?

8 What is the largest member of the violin family?

9 How many strings does a violin have?

10 Which composer died at the age of 35?

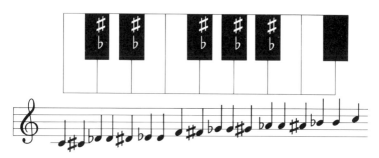

■ WHY DO HUMAN BEINGS MAKE MUSIC?

Music is one of the most important ways of giving expression to our thoughts and feelings. Even if no words are sung, it can still be a dramatic way of expressing our emotions.

Music is a way of blending sounds that are made up of three basic parts – rhythm, harmony and melody. These ingredients may be used on their own, or they may be combined in endless ways.

■ WHEN WERE MUSICAL INSTRUMENTS FIRST PLAYED?

Musical instruments have been played since prehistoric times. The earliest instruments were objects such as conches (seashells) and bone pipes.

QUIZ 3

1 Which composer was deaf for half his life?
2 Which instrument does James Galway play?
3 Which instrument does Yehudi Menuhin play?
4 What are the words of a song called?
5 Who wrote The Planets?
6 Who wrote Pomp and Circumstance?
7 In music, what does 'adagio' mean?
8 Where are panpipes played?
9 What instrument did Louis Armstrong play?
10 In myth, what instrument did Orpheus play?

Later, instruments were made from materials such as wood and pottery. People found that string can make a musical note when stretched tight, so they made the first musical bow. The picture shows musicians of ancient Egypt.

FOR WHOM DID VIVALDI COMPOSE HIS MUSIC?

Antonio Vivaldi, the Italian composer who lived from 1678 to 1741, composed most of his music for the pupils of a girls' orphanage in Venice.

The orphanage was the Conservatorio della Pietá. His job was to teach the violin, but because the choir and orchestra were so good, he composed music for them. Vivaldi's most famous work includes the four *Four Seasons* concertos, but he wrote hundreds of other pieces.

QUIZ 4

1 What instrument is associated with Wales?
2 Where are balalaikas played?
3 What are tom-toms and timpani?
4 What instrument is a plectrum used to play?
5 What were Mozart's first names?
6 Who was Benjamin Britten?
7 Who wrote the Moonlight Sonata?
8 Who wrote the Four Seasons?
9 Which piano composer was Polish?
10 What are La Traviata and Aida?

WHO WAS JOHANN SEBASTIAN BACH?

Johann Sebastian Bach (1685–1750) was the most famous member of a family of musicians from the German town of Eisenach.

Bach composed his famous work, the Brandenburg Concertos, whilst working as musical director to Prince Leopold of Kothen.

Bach had trained as a church organist and wrote a lot of church music, including 200 cantatas (music to be sung), as well as a *Mass in B Minor*. He also wrote three settings of the Passion story, the most famous of which is his *St Matthew Passion*. Tragically, in 1747, Bach went blind. He died soon afterwards.

PEOPLE & PLACES

■ WHO WAS MOZART?

Wolfgang Amadeus Mozart (1756–1791) lived for only 35 years, but in that time he became one of the world's most famous composers.

Mozart began composing at the age of five. As a child he could play the harpsichord and violin extremely well. Mozart's work included many concertos for a variety of instruments. He also wrote symphonies and several great operas, including *The Marriage of Figaro*, *The Magic Flute*, *Don Giovanni* and *Cosí fan tutte*.

QUIZ 5

1 What did Stradivarius make?
2 Who wrote words to Sullivan's music?
3 Where is The Mikado *set*?
4 What nationality was the composer Wagner?
5 Where in London are the Proms held?
6 What is a conductor's stick called?
7 What sort of instruments are oboes and flutes?
8 Who wrote the Brandenburg Concerto?
9 What instruments have pick-ups?
10 Where were sitars first played?

■ WHO WAS BEETHOVEN?

Ludwig van Beethoven (1770–1827) has been called the greatest composer who has ever lived – yet he was deaf for much of his life.

Beethoven was born in Bonn in Germany. He studied under Mozart and later with Josef Haydn. He is remembered for many great works, including masterpieces such as the *Moonlight Sonata*, the *Emperor Concerto* and his famous *Ninth Symphony,* in which he introduced choral music for the first time in a symphony.

WHO WAS TCHAIKOVSKY?

The Russian composer Peter Ilich Tchaikovsky (1840–1893) is probably best known as the composer of ballet music, though he wrote many other pieces.

In 1877 Tchaikovsky was given an allowance from a wealthy widow on condition that they never met! He then began to compose most of his major works. Some of his most popular compositions include the ballets *Sleeping Beauty* and *Swan Lake*, and the *Romeo and Juliet* overture and the opera *Eugene Onegin*.

QUIZ 6

1 Which Dutch artist chopped off his ear?

2 Which French artist is famous for his posters?

3 Who sculpted the famous statue of David?

4 What nationality was Salvador Dali?

5 Which artist had a Blue Period?

6 Who painted the famous picture of the Mona Lisa?

7 In which gallery is the Mona Lisa kept?

8 What nationality was Leonardo da Vinci?

9 Which famous statue has no arms?

10 Who painted The Haywain?

WHO WAS STRAVINSKY?

Igor Stravinsky (1882–1971) was a Russian composer. He wrote dramatic ballet music.

In 1909 Stravinsky spent a season working in Paris with the famous *Ballets Russes*. He wrote several scores for the ballet, including *The Firebird* and *The Rite of Spring*. The last composition caused uproar at first, but today it is recognised as one of Stravinsky's best works.

PEOPLE & PLACES

WHEN WAS OPERA FIRST PERFORMED?

The beginning of opera is usually dated around 1600 in Italy, when stage plays set to music were first performed.

Works of drama performed to music existed long ago, for example in the Mystery, Miracle and Morality plays of the Middle Ages. The first full stage play set to music, in which the characters sing, was produced in 1597. Its music has not survived. The first two surviving operas were performed in 1600 in Italy. Both had specially designed costumes, scenery, lighting and stage machinery.

WHEN WAS JAZZ FIRST PLAYED?

The style of music known as jazz emerged at the start of the 20th century. It began in the southern states of the USA among black musicians.

By the start of the 1900s a distinct type of music had developed in New Orleans, in Louisiana. The early leaders of this 'jazz' music were all trumpeters, including Louis Armstrong.

QUIZ 7

1 What type of painting is an aquarelle?

2 What nationality was the painter Renoir?

3 What do painters use to hold their canvases?

4 What are artists' workshops called?

5 What sort of artist was Henry Moore?

6 Which 19th-century painter painted sunflowers?

7 What nationality was Degas?

8 What nationality was Gainsborough?

9 What are pictures of places called?

10 What are pictures of people called?

WHERE WAS THE POTTER'S WHEEL INVENTED?

Pottery was one of the earliest inventions. At first pots were shaped by hand out of wet clay. Turning pots on a wheel came later.

The wheel was invented in Sumeria, Babylon and elsewhere in the Near East around 3000 BC. The invention of the potter's wheel led to one of the first industries – pottery. A skilful potter could make enough pots to exchange them for food and other goods, or sell them for money.

QUIZ 8

1 What does Tom Stoppard write?

2 Where was Shakespeare born?

3 Who did Shakespeare marry?

4 Where was the Globe Theatre?

5 Who is Romeo's girlfriend?

6 What nationality was George Bernard Shaw?

7 In what sort of play would you find a dame?

8 Which pantomime features Widow Twankey?

9 In what century were pantomimes most popular?

10 Who wrote Macbeth?

WHO WAS PHIDEAS?

Phideas was a sculptor in Ancient Greece. Very little of his work survives today, yet his fame has lasted until modern times.

It is thought that Phideas lived from about 490 to 430 BC. The ruler of Athens, Pericles, put him in charge of an important building programme which included the sculptures of the Parthenon. Phideas made a huge gold and ivory statue of the goddess Athena which, at about 10 metres tall, was the largest statue ever erected in Athens. A later, bronze statue of Athena was even taller – but because he put his own portrait as well as Pericles's on her shield, he was accused of irreverence and sent into exile.

PEOPLE & PLACES

WHO WAS PIERO DELLA FRANCESCA?

Piero della Francesca was one of the most important artists of the Italian Renaissance. He is best known for his clear, lifelike pictures, though in his own day he was more famous for his scientific work and he did not have much influence on other painters of his time.

He was born in 1420, and died in 1492. Like other Renaissance artists, he had wide interests. He was especially concerned with geometry, which he used to help him work out the basic patterns for his pictures and get the perspective right. His work was often in the form of frescoes.

QUIZ 9

1 Where was Hamlet a prince?

2 Which Shakespearian king asked for a horse?

3 Which Egyptian queen did Shakespeare write of?

4 Who was Othello's wife?

5 Who was the Merchant of Venice?

6 Who was Lawrence Olivier?

7 In A Midsummer Night's Dream who is the weaver?

8 In A Midsummer Night's Dream who is Puck?

9 What play is about the Montagues and Capulets?

10 In which book do the Darling family appear?

WHO WAS MICHELANGELO?

Michelangelo (1475–1564) is often said to be one of the greatest artists Europe has ever produced. He was certainly one of the most important figures in the Italian Renaissance.

Michelangelo Buonarroti's best known work includes some magnificent sculpture, such as his *Pietá,* and his statue of the young Biblical king, *David.* He is also famous for the frescoes of the Sistine Chapel, in the Vatican in Rome.

WHO WAS LEONARDO DA VINCI?

Leonardo (1452–1519) was one of the world's most talented people. He was a painter, sculptor, architect, anatomist, scientist, inventor, engineer and musician.

This extraordinary Italian was a leading figure of the Renaissance, the rebirth of learning. He began many projects, but finished only a few. His artistic masterpiece is the wall painting of the Last Supper at a monastery in Milan. He is noted for his advanced knowledge of anatomy.

WHY IS THE MONA LISA SMILING?

The gentle smile of La Gioconda, or Mona Lisa, as she is often known, has made this painting one of Leonardo da Vinci's most famous. While he painted her portrait, Leonardo used musicians, singers and jesters to keep her in a merry mood.

The pleasure reflected in Mona Lisa's face was captured with great skill by Leonardo. The painting seems to be as alive as the beautiful woman who sat for it. Although Leonardo worked on the painting for over four years, he eventually left it unfinished.

QUIZ 10

1 What is a picture house?

2 What was the first talking movie called?

3 What was Charlie Chaplin famous as?

4 What type of movie did John Wayne make?

5 Who changed her name from Norma Jean?

6 Where is Hollywood?

7 Who starred in Mary Poppins?

8 Which cartoon mouse was created by Walt Disney?

9 What temple did Indiana Jones explore?

10 Who played Indiana Jones in the films?

PEOPLE & PLACES

WHO MADE THE FIRST OIL PAINTINGS?

Strictly speaking, we do not know who made the first oil paintings, since the technique goes back to the Middle Ages. But we do know that the Flemish painters Hubert and Jan van Eyck, who were painting around the 1420s, were the first to make the most of the possibilities the method offers in terms of depth and shades of colour.

We are not sure what new method the van Eycks brought to oil painting, but they were famous in their own time for their entirely new techniques.

WHO WERE KNOWN AS THE POST-IMPRESSIONISTS?

QUIZ 11

1 Who was Batman's main enemy?

2 Who was Batman's friend?

3 What is an Oscar?

4 In which film does Dorothy wear red shoes?

5 What were the first films with sound called?

6 Which secret agent has code name 007?

7 Who wrote the books about 007?

8 Who devises all 007's special equipment?

9 What were Laurel and Hardy's first names?

10 Which films had a hero called Luke Skywalker?

The Post-Impressionists is the name given to the group of artists, working mainly in France, whose work followed the Impressionist movement of the 19th century. The name, given to the work of Seurat, Gauguin, Van Gogh and Cézanne, comes from the title of an exhibition in 1910 called **Manet and the Post-Impressionists**.

Although these artists have been grouped together as Post-Impressionists, their work is very different.

WHEN WAS PERSPECTIVE FIRST USED IN EUROPEAN PAINTING?

Perspective is a method of drawing a picture so as to give an impression of realistic depth and distance. The laws of perspective were worked out and first used in the 15th century in Italy.

The Italian architect Brunelleschi worked out the principles of perspective. These are based on the fact that objects seem smaller the closer they are to the horizon. Brunelleschi's friend Masaccio first applied these ideas to painting in a fresco (wall painting) finished in 1427. The use of perspective gave a totally new approach to painting. It was followed by European artists for 500 years.

QUIZ 12

1 On what space ship does Mr Spock fly?

2 Who is Mr Spock's captain?

3 In the film, what is Chitty Chitty Bang Bang?

4 Who rode a horse called Silver?

5 What sort of film does an animator create?

6 Which cartoon duck has three nephews?

7 Which cartoon features a cat and mouse?

8 Which male actor starred in Casablanca?

9 Which film featured Scarlett O'Hara?

10 Who played the Godfather?

WHEN WERE THE FIRST WATERCOLOURS PAINTED?

The use of watercolour in painting has a long history. We know that watercolour paint was used on papyrus rolls in ancient Egypt, and in the earliest paintings of China.

Watercolour is a paint ground in gum (usually gum arabic), which can be dissolved in water. It is usually applied with a brush. Drawings in watercolour and ink have been the basis of Chinese art since the beginning of the T'ang Dynasty in AD 618.

PEOPLE & PLACES

WHO WAS PICASSO?

Pablo Ruiz y Picasso (1881–1973) was a Spanish artist who lived mostly in France. He must be the best known of all 20th-century painters. He painted in several different styles, and greatly influenced other painters.

Picasso's early work was done mainly in blue. Later, he worked on pictures showing figures as fragments of geometric shapes – the style we know as cubism.
One of Picasso's most famous pictures is *Guernica,* which depicts the destruction of a town during the Spanish civil war.

QUIZ 13

1 What are marionnettes?

2 What is Punch's puppet wife called?

3 Who might use the word 'abracadabra'?

4 What was Joseph Grimaldi's profession?

5 Who introduces the acts at a circus?

6 Which circus act shows great balance?

7 What is a ventriloquist's doll called?

8 What game did Gary Kasparov play?

9 How many cards are there in a deck?

10 What is a matador?

WHY ARE SOME PAINTINGS CALLED ABSTRACT?

Paintings in which the subject is not obvious or in which the artist has made no effort to show real objects are known as abstract paintings. They may contain lines, colours and shapes, but these do not form a recognizable object or person.

Abstract art is one way for a painter to leave aside the appearance of things, and search for the deeper truth that may lie inside them. This might be the difference between showing the beauty of a face and showing that all mankind is mortal.

WHEN WERE THE FIRST SCULPTURES MADE?

The earliest sculptures that have been found are as much as 30,000 years old, dating from the Stone Age. They are tiny figures representing women, which have come to be known as the 'Venuses'.

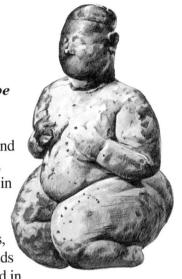

Stone Age Venuses have been found all over Europe and Western Asia, from the Pyrenees to Lake Baikal in Russia. Stone Age sculptors also made figures of animals. These included mammoths, rhinoceroses, horses, cave bears and various kinds of cat. Stone Age sculptors worked in a variety of materials. They used ivory, bone and stone such as limestone and sandstone.

QUIZ 14

1 What religion worships in mosques?

2 What religion worships in synagogues?

3 What religion uses prayer wheels?

4 What religion has bar mitzvah ceremonies?

5 Who lives at the Vatican?

6 Where did the Dalai Lama rule?

7 Which religious group did Joseph Smith set up?

8 What is the first book of the Bible?

9 What is the last book of the Bible?

10 What does 'Islam' mean?

WHO WAS RODIN?

Auguste Rodin (1840–1917) was a French sculptor whose work, often large figures cast in bronze, includes **The Thinker** *and* **The Kiss**.

In 1878 Rodin held an exhibition of his work in which his figures were so lifelike that he was accused of casting them from live models. He enjoyed conveying a feeling of movement in his work – many of his models were dancers.

PEOPLE & PLACES

■ WHERE HAVE ANCIENT TEMPLES BEEN DISMANTLED AND REBUILT?

When the High Dam was built at Aswan on the River Nile, a great lake formed behind it. To prevent the water engulfing them, two temples at Abu Simbel were dismantled and rebuilt on higher ground.

The Egyptian Pharaoh Ramses II had the temples built at Abu Simbel about 3200 years ago. They were carved out of the face of a cliff beside the River Nile. The Great Temple had 14 rooms and stretched 60 metres into the cliff. Four huge stone seated figures guarded the other temple.

■ WHERE IS THE VALLEY OF THE KINGS?

This is a narrow rocky gorge on the west bank of the River Nile in southern Egypt. Ancient Egyptians buried many of their kings in the valley.

The Valley of the Kings lies near the ancient Egyptian city of Thebes. Here, in the desert, people have discovered more than 60 tombs. They were made more than 3200 years ago.

Each tomb consists of corridors and rooms cut deep into solid rock. Sculptors and artists carved and painted religious signs and writing on the walls. Deep pits were built to keep out robbers.

QUIZ 15

1 What is esperanto?
2 Who invented the mechanical printing press?
3 What is a book of maps called?
4 What sort of stories did Aesop write?
5 According to Aesop, who did the tortoise beat?
6 What is a sonnet?
7 Who is the most famous Scottish poet?
8 What was Wordsworth's Christian name?
9 What did Wordsworth write poetry about?
10 What region of Britain did Wordsworth write about?

WHERE WERE ROADS FIRST PAVED?

When people first began to travel, they followed rough tracks and trails. In bad weather, it was safer to stay at home. Paved roads were not thought of until wheeled carts came into use.

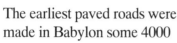

The earliest paved roads were made in Babylon some 4000 years ago. As people began living in towns and trading with their neighbours, they needed better transport.

Many ancient cities had paved roads, and we can still see their remains today. But undoubtedly the greatest road-builders of the past were the Romans.

WHAT WAS THE COLOSSEUM BUILT FOR?

The Colosseum was a huge stadium in ancient Rome. Crowds flocked there to see the 'games', at which there were fights and other bloody contests.

Inside stadiums like the Colosseum, audiences of 80,000 or more could sit in tiers around the arena. The contests took place in the arena, which was like a circus ring. The arena could even be flooded to stage mock sea-battles! Romans liked cruel sports. Animals were kept in pens underneath the arena. They were matched against men or other animals. Specially trained fighters, known as gladiators, fought to the death. They were armed with swords and spears.

QUIZ 16

1 What nationality was the poet W.B. Yeats?
2 In the poem, who did Minnehaha marry?
3 Who is the Poet Laureate?
4 Who created Skimbleshanks the cat?
5 What musical does Skimbleshanks appear in?
6 Where is Poets' Corner?
7 Where does Haiku poetry come from?
8 What bird did the ancient mariner kill?
9 Who was famous for his nonsense verse?
10 In the poem, who had a luminous nose?

◼ WHAT IS A MYSTERY PLAY?

Mystery plays were plays about Bible stories or saints' lives. They were performed outdoors in the Middle Ages.

'Mystery' comes from the Latin word *ministerium,* meaning 'religious service'. The first mystery plays were acted by priests at services in churches. Later, tradesmen, craftsmen and other groups put on plays outside churches. A group of plays would be performed at festivals such as Easter or Christmas. Between them, the plays told all the important Bible stories in a lively, enjoyable way.

QUIZ 17
1 Who wrote the book Little Women?
2 What sex was the writer George Eliot?
3 Did Sherlock Holmes really exist?
4 Who was Sherlock Holmes' companion?
5 Where did Sherlock Holmes live?
6 Who was Sherlock Holmes' main enemy?
7 Who were Porthos, Athos and Aramis?
8 Who did Friday become friendly with?
9 What type of creature was Bilbo Baggins?
10 Who was the wizard in The Hobbit?

◼ WHAT IS KABUKI?

Kabuki is the name for a type of play performed in Japan. Its name means 'the art of singing and dancing'. Kabuki plays contain plenty of both.

Many kabuki plays are about a string of exciting events, some of them magical. Actors wear elaborate costumes and their faces are heavily painted. Heroes are white but villains are reddish. The actors, all men, often fight pretended duels, and mime actions such as drinking tea from invisible cups. Music is played all through each drama and the actors sing, rather like opera singers.

WHAT IS A MIME?

A mime is a silent play, or acting without words. Actors show what they mean by gestures and facial expressions instead of spoken words. Actors who work like this are also called mimes.

Modern mime acting began in the 1800s in France. The first great French mime was Jean-Baptiste-Gaspard Deburau, who died in 1846. Today, mimes imitate actions such as climbing stairs, cleaning windows or chasing a butterfly.

WHO WROTE THE FIRST TRAGEDIES?

Tragedy is a kind of drama that grew up in Ancient Greece. Among the early writers of tragedy, the best known are Aeschylus, Sophocles and Euripides.

Until Aeschylus, plays were for one actor and a chorus. Aeschylus introduced a second actor to his plays. Sophocles made more changes to the traditional style. Euripides wrote many violent plays, but in later life he wrote tragi-comedies with happy endings. This started a new trend in Greek drama.

QUIZ 18

1 What famous sisters lived at Howarth, Yorkshire?

2 In what book does Heathcliffe appear?

3 Which character slept for 20 years?

4 Who visited Lilliput?

5 Who wrote Tom Sawyer and Huckleberry Finn?

6 Who wrote the Narnia chronicles?

7 What was the lion called in the Narnia books?

8 Who wrote Peter Pan?

9 What is the name of the fairy in Peter Pan?

10 Who is the pirate captain in Peter Pan?

PEOPLE & PLACES

QUIZ 19

1 Who wrote Nicholas Nickleby?

2 Which novel does Mr Pickwick feature in?

3 Which novel does Scrooge feature in?

4 How many ghosts visit Scrooge?

5 Which Dickens orphan asked for "more"?

6 Who wrote The Waterbabies?

7 Which Swiss family were shipwrecked?

8 Who is the hero of Treasure Island?

9 Who is the pirate leader in Treasure Island?

10 Who wrote Kidnapped?

WHO WAS ANTON CHEKHOV?

Anton Chekhov (1860–1904) was a Russian playwright and writer of short stories. Among his best known works are the plays Uncle Vanya *and* The Seagull. *His plays are often about the decline of the Russian land-owning class.*

As a young man Chekhov trained as a doctor, and supported himself and his family by writing comic sketches for magazines. He later built up a reputation as a dramatist and short-story writer.

WHO WAS WILLIAM SHAKESPEARE?

William Shakespeare (1564–1616) was one of the world's greatest dramatists and his 35 plays remain the most important drama ever written in English.

Shakespeare was born in Stratford-upon-Avon but moved to London. There he became an actor and a director, writing plays for his company to perform, and probably producing them too. His plays cover a wide variety of subject matter and include histories, light comedies such as *A Midsummer Night's Dream* , shown right, and dark tragedies such as *Hamlet* and *King Lear*. As well as writing plays, he was also a poet.

WHO ARE COLUMBINE AND HARLEQUIN?

Columbine and Harlequin are two main characters in the Commedia dell'arte *– a form of traditional theatre that started in Italy at the end of the Renaissance. It was popular all over Europe until the 18th century.*

Commedia dell'arte was based on very simple plots – usually involving young lovers whose parents do not want them to marry, and a group of witty and intelligent servants, who help them. Into this action, entertainment such as acrobatics, juggling and music were added. The characters of Harlequin and Columbine developed from the French form of this theatre.

QUIZ 20

1 Where was the Railway Children's father?
2 Who went around the world in 80 days?
3 Who accompanied him?
4 Which book featured blind Mr Rochester?
5 Who was bullied by Flashman?
6 What school did Flashman attend?
7 Who discovered a midnight garden?
8 Who lived at Green Gables?
9 Who lived at Sunnybrook Farm?
10 What sort of books did Georgette Heyer write?

WHO SOLD HIS SOUL TO THE DEVIL?

There is a German legend, dating back to the 16th century, about a magician named Faust who sold his

soul to the devil in return for knowledge and power. An important version of the story is by the writer Johann Wolfgang von Goethe.

Goethe's story – published in 1808 and 1832 – is different from earlier versions (such as that by the English playwright, Christopher Marlowe) since Faust is saved instead of going to hell.

PEOPLE & PLACES

WHO WAS BERTOLT BRECHT?

Bertolt Brecht (1898–1956) was a German playwright who had an important influence on 20th-century drama. He developed a theory of drama whereby the audience was made to criticise, instead of identifying with, the characters.

Many of Brecht's plays were socialist, including *The Threepenny Opera*, which had music by the German composer Kurt Weill. With the rise of Hitler, Brecht was forced to leave Germany. He wrote his most famous work, *The Caucasian Chalk Circle*, in the United States. In 1949 he returned to Germany, where he ran a theatre.

QUIZ 21

1 What is Wurzel Gummidge?
2 Who is the child in The Jungle Book?
3 What bear befriends him?
4 What is Christopher Robin's bear called?
5 What sort of animal is Eeyore?
6 Who wrote Charlie and the Chocolate Factory?
7 Who owned the chocolate factory?
8 Where did Alice have adventures?
9 Who was Tweedledee's twin brother?
10 Who wrote the Famous Five stories?

WHO WAS MOLIERE?

Moliere (1622–1673) was a French writer and great comic dramatist. Among his best known works are Tartuffe, Le Misanthrope *and* Le Bourgeois Gentilhomme.

Moliere – whose real name was Jean-Baptiste Poquelin – was a brilliant comic actor and took part in his own plays. But his work often offended the Church. One of his best known works is *Tartuffe* about a hypocritical religious man who is eventually unmasked. The play was banned for five years. In the end it was a great success.

WHY DO FILMS HAVE DIRECTORS?

The director of a film has the same task as the conductor of an orchestra. He rehearses the actors and helps them to interpret their parts. Directors must also work from a raw script and assemble from it all the parts that go into making a finished production.

One very important thing is the way a film looks to the audience. The director works with designers, lighting and sound crews to make the stage sets look authentic.

QUIZ 22

1 Who lived at Toad Hall?

2 In what book does Toad Hall appear?

3 What did Thomas Hardy write?

4 How many thieves did Ali Baba outwit?

5 What sort of books did Agatha Christie write?

6 What nationality was Hercule Poirot?

7 Who was Agatha Christie's female sleuth?

8 What train did Agatha Christie write of?

9 Where did the Pied Piper live?

10 Who was Sinbad?

WHY DO ACTORS WEAR MAKE-UP?

Actors use make-up when they are performing in order to look more 'natural' or else to change their appearance to suit the part they are playing.

Make-up can improve on nature or disguise it entirely. Theatre actors may wear thick make-up to highlight their eyes and lips and features which might otherwise be washed out by the powerful stage lights. For example, a blonde actress can be made to look blonder still if she wears dark make-up on her face. A villain, however, looks more evil if the eyebrows are made heavier and closer.

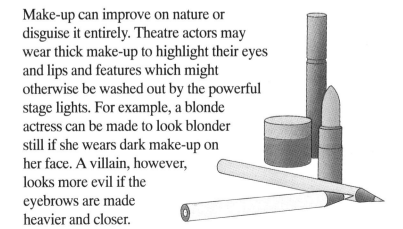

PEOPLE & PLACES

WHY DO CIRCUSES HAVE CLOWNS?

The lure of the circus is its spectacular displays of human skill and daring which amaze and thrill the crowds. When the excitement becomes too great for the audience, it is eased by the clowns. By making the spectators laugh, the clowns help them to relax again.

Oleg Popov of the Moscow Circus is one of the greatest clowns ever to have worked in the circus.

The role he plays is that of the simple bumpkin trying to copy the great riders and acrobats. His efforts to imitate their acts almost seem to succeed. But in the end they are always bungled!

QUIZ 23

1 *In which book are Piggy and Ralph shipwrecked?*

2 *Where does Stig live?*

3 *Who was Dr Doolittle able to talk to?*

4 *Who wrote the Swallows and Amazons series?*

5 *What was special about Frances Burnett's garden?*

6 *Who wrote* Black Beauty*?*

7 *What school did Billy Bunter go to?*

8 *What was Billy Bunter's favourite hobby?*

9 *Who created* Jeremy Fisher *and* Peter Rabbit*?*

10 *What type of animal was Mrs Tiggywinkle?*

WHY DO TIGHT-ROPE WALKERS SOMETIMES CARRY LONG POLES?

A long pole helps a tight-rope walker to balance while crossing the rope. It has the same effect as holding out one's arms when walking along a narrow plank.

Not all tightrope artists use poles however. Some of the greatest performed all kinds of amazing feats without ever using them.

WHERE DO PUPPETS COME FROM?

Puppets were known long ago in ancient Greece and Egypt. They were always a very popular form of entertainment and were used to tell legends and folk tales.

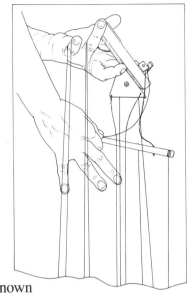

In Italy in the 16th century puppet shows were regular events. A hero called Pulcinello was based on a character who was popular in theatres of the time. In England, Pulcinello became known as Punch and Punch and Judy shows became popular.

QUIZ 24

1 What subject does a linguist study?

2 What kind of things does a cooper make?

3 Who might use an anvil to make shoes?

4 Who wear wimples?

5 What do the initials V.I.P. stand for?

6 What does a lexicographer write?

7 What does a philatelist collect?

8 What does a milliner make?

9 What does a campanologist ring?

10 What material do carpenters work with?

HOW DO VENTRILOQUISTS 'THROW' THEIR VOICES?

Ventriloquists do not 'throw' their voices; they simply talk without moving their lips. An audience may think that the voice is coming from somewhere else.

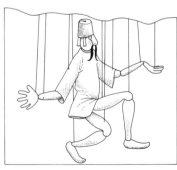

The ventriloquist forms words in a normal way but then breathes out very slowly and muffles the sounds by tightening his throat. Usually the spectators' imaginations will fool them into believing that the dummy is speaking.

WHY DO MAGICIANS USE PROPS?

Stage magicians use props such as tall hats, magic wands, scarves and capes as they practise a kind of magic based on 'sleight of hand' and other tricks.

Stage magic is only meant for entertainment. If it is well performed it gives the impression that the tricks are truly magical, not simply the clever manipulation of objects.

WHY DO PEOPLE READ HOROSCOPES?

The movements of the major heavenly bodies are believed by some people to shape human affairs and to influence human character. Horoscopes are intended to help us understand how these movements affect our everyday lives.

Astrologers plot a person's horoscope from the time of birth in order to understand their nature, and to learn about their future. Many people read their horoscope every day.

QUIZ 25

1 What is the currency of the USA?

2 What is the currency of France?

3 What is the currency of Russia?

4 What is the currency of Holland?

5 What is the currency of Mexico?

6 Where do people pay with yen?

7 Where do people pay with deutschmarks?

8 Where do people pay with pesetas?

9 Where do people pay with lira?

10 Where do people pay with rupees?

WHEN DID PEOPLE FIRST USE MONEY?

Today we use money to buy things. But when trade began thousands of years ago, there was no money. So people exchanged goods. The invention of money made trade much simpler.

The first metal coins were minted (made) in about 800 BC. Metal coins, especially gold and silver ones, have real value, but paper money is merely a token. The paper is worthless. Paper money was used in China by AD 800.

QUIZ 26

1 What country is associated with sombreros?

2 What country is famous for cuckoo clocks?

3 In which country would you find dykes?

4 In what country do women wear saris?

5 What country is associated with shamrock?

6 Where might you find an eisteddfod?

7 What country is famous for bullfighting?

8 What country is associated with boomerangs?

9 In what country do men wear kilts?

10 Where do women wear kimonos?

WHEN WERE POSTAGE STAMPS FIRST USED?

Adhesive postage stamps first came into use in Britain in 1840. Stamps made it easier and cheaper for people to send letters.

In the early 1800s Rowland Hill saw that it would save time if letters could be sent any distance for a fixed charge. In 1840 the 'penny post' was first used. The method was simple. The sender bought a postage stamp and stuck it on the letter.

PEOPLE & PLACES

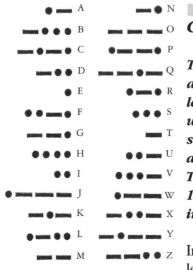

WHAT IS MORSE CODE?

This is a code using dots and dashes to stand for letters and numbers. It was once the main way of sending telegraph signals along wires or by radio. The code was invented in 1837 by the American inventor Samuel Morse.

In Morse code, different letters, numbers and punctuation marks are given as different groups of dots and dashes. Dots are sent as short signals, dashes as long signals. Signals are made by pressing the key of a sending device which alters a continuous electrical or radio signal and produces rapid sounds in a receiver.

WHAT IS SEMAPHORE USED FOR?

Semaphore is a method of using flags or mechanical arms or lights to signal messages. Its name comes from two Greek words meaning 'signal carrier'.

Semaphore signalling was invented as a way of sending signals between people who could see one another but were out of earshot. Sailors use semaphore to signal from ship to ship when they are afraid their radio signals might be overheard by an enemy. A signaller holds two flags or lights at arm's length and moves his arms to different positions, like the hands on a clock. Each position stands for a different letter of the alphabet.

QUIZ 27

1 What is the capital of Guatemala?

2 Where is the Outback?

3 What is the capital of Argentina?

4 What is the river called that runs through Paris?

5 What is the most sacred Indian river?

6 What is the capital of Iceland?

7 What country is known as The Emerald Isle?

8 Where would you find gondoliers?

9 What is the capital of Honduras?

10 Which Irish stone do people kiss?

WHAT IS DEAF-AND-DUMB LANGUAGE?

Deaf-and-dumb language is a way of 'talking' with the fingers and hands instead of the mouth. People who are unable to speak or hear can use it to hold conversations.

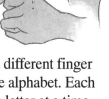

There are two main kinds of deaf-and-dumb language. One method uses one hand, the other uses both hands. In both methods, different finger positions stand for different letters of the alphabet. Each method involves spelling out words one letter at a time. Talking in deaf-and-dumb sign language is much slower than speaking. Deaf-and-dumb people can talk faster if they also use other gestures and facial expressions as short cuts.

WHAT IS BRAILLE?

Braille is a code of raised dots. Blind people can read Braille by running their fingers over the dots on a page. The code was invented in the 1820s by a blind student called Louis Braille.

> **QUIZ 28**
>
> 1 What is the capital of Belgium?
> 2 What river runs through London?
> 3 Where is Kilimanjaro?
> 4 What is the capital of New Zealand?
> 5 Where are the Angel Falls?
> 6 Where are the Seychelles?
> 7 What is the American flag called?
> 8 What is the British flag called?
> 9 What constellation is on Australia's flag?
> 10 What is the name of France's flag?

Braille produced 63 different dot patterns standing for different letters, punctuation marks, numbers and even musical notes. People can also type Braille.

PEOPLE & PLACES

■ WHAT ARE HIEROGLYPHICS?

The ancient Egyptians used a complicated kind of sign-writing. The Greeks called these signs 'hieroglyphs' (sacred writing). For centuries experts puzzled over the meaning of the hieroglyphs on temples and tombs.

Hieroglyphics was a more advanced version of the picture-writing the Egyptians first used.
No one could read this ancient script until 1799, when a tablet, called the Rosetta Stone, was discovered. It had the same inscription in three forms of writing: hieroglyphics, Coptic Egyptian and Greek. Because the last two were understood, it was possible to decipher the hieroglyphics.

■ WHERE WAS THE FIRST BOOK PRINTED?

The Chinese were the first people to print books on paper. They used wood blocks for this. Much later, the mechanical printing press was invented.

The earliest known printed book was made around AD 868. It is called the Diamond Sutra and was hand-printed, using wooden blocks. This printing method is slow. Even so, it is faster than copying books by hand. In Europe, at that time, all books were copied by hand – usually by monks. Books were so precious that they were often chained to reading stands. Modern printing did not begin in Europe until the 1440s.

QUIZ 29

1 How many events are there in a decathlon?
2 How often do the Olympic Games take place?
3 What sport do the Harlem Globetrotters play?
4 In what sports would you find a bullseye?
5 How many players are there in a soccer team?
6 What sport are Torvill and Dean famous for?
7 In what sport would you play with shuttlecocks?
8 What sport is Muhammad Ali famous for?
9 In what sport would you find a linebacker?
10 What is speedway?

■ WHERE WERE THE FIRST UNIVERSITIES FOUNDED?

A university is a place of 'all learning'. New knowledge in the Middle Ages led to the setting up of great centres of learning throughout Europe. Many of these universities are still in existence today.

By the 1300s, knowledge was growing rapidly. For centuries education had been left to the Church. Now, all over Europe, universities came into being. Great universities were founded in cities such as Paris, Bologna, Oxford, Cambridge and Prague. The only subjects taught at first were law, theology (religion) and medicine. One of the first medical schools was founded in the 9th century at the university of Salerno in Italy.

QUIZ 30

1 In what sport might you use a 3 iron?

2 What sport takes place at Aintree?

3 What sportsmen enter the Tour de France?

4 What does the leader of the race wear?

5 How many people form a netball team?

6 Was Sebastian Coe a track or field eventer?

7 What races at drag races?

8 Where is bowls played?

9 What sport has the Admiral's Cup?

10 What sport uses foils and epées?

■ WHEN WERE THE FIRST NEWSPAPERS PUBLISHED?

People began reading newspapers in the 1600s. Until then, news had travelled slowly by word of mouth.

In the 1500s, after the invention of printing machinery, people began reading pamphlets and newsletters. The first newspaper to be printed regularly was called the *Corante*. It came out in London in 1621 and contained news from France, Italy, Spain and other countries.

Newspapers quickly became popular. In 1643 the first paper with pictures appeared. Its title was the *Civic Mercury*. By the 1700s, newspapers carried news of world events, business, shipping, farm prices, theatre and gossip.

PEOPLE & PLACES

WHO WAS OMAR KHAYYAM?

Omar Khayyam was a Persian poet, astronomer and a brilliant scholar who lived in the 11th century. He is most famous as a poet, and a collection of his work, called the Rubaiyat, was translated into English in the 19th century.

In his own day, Omar Khayyam was famous as a writer on science, history, law, medicine and, especially, mathematics. The *Rubaiyat* was only published 200 years after his death.

QUIZ 31

1 How many events are there in a decathlon?
2 How often do the Olympic Games take place?
3 What sport do the Harlem Globetrotters play?
4 In what sports would you find a bullseye?
5 How many players are there in a soccer team?
6 What sport are Torvill and Dean famous for?
7 What sport uses shuttlecocks?
8 What sport is Muhammad Ali famous for?
9 In what sport would you find a linebacker?
10 What is speedway?

WHO WROTE THE TALE OF GENJI?

The Tale of Genji *is an 11th-century book from Japan which is sometimes said to be the very first novel ever written. Its author was a woman – Murasaki Shikibu.*

The book was written in about 1010 and was an immediate success. It was popular for centuries afterwards. The story is of the life and loves of Prince Genji. He loves several women, and each one reacts differently to him.

WHO TOLD STORIES FOR 1001 NIGHTS?

There was once a princess Sharazad in Arabia who saved herself from death by telling stories for 1001 nights.

The story tells of a cruel king who married a new wife every day and had her put to death. On Sharazad's wedding night, she began to tell the king a story. But when she reached the most exciting part, she said if he wanted to hear the end he would have to let her live another day. Among the stories that Sharazad told were those of *Sinbad the Sailor* and *Aladdin*.

QUIZ 32

1 In what sport might you use a 3 iron?

2 What sport takes place at Aintree?

3 What sportsmen enter the Tour de France?

4 What does the leader of the race wear?

5 How many people form a netball team?

6 Was Sebastian Coe a track or field eventer?

7 What races at drag races?

8 Where is bowls played?

9 What sport has the Admiral's Cup?

10 What sport uses foils and epées?

WHO WROTE THE DIVINE COMEDY?

The Divine Comedy – which many scholars think is one of the most important pieces of literature produced in medieval Europe – was written by the poet Dante Aligheri in his own language, Italian.

The poem was finished around 1321. It was written in three parts. The poem describes an imaginary journey in which the poet – Dante himself – visits Hell, Purgatory and finally Heaven.

WHO WAS PETRARCH?

Petrarch (1304–1374) was an Italian poet who had an enormous influence on European poetry.

Petrarch's full name was Francesco Petrarca. He wrote more than 400 poems of his own. Many of these are written to a woman called Laura. He set out firm rules for writing poetry, including the number of lines to be used. He spent much of his life researching Latin poetry and it is thanks to his work that the poetry of the Romans Livy and Cicero was rediscovered.

QUIZ 33

1 What sport takes place at Brands Hatch?

2 What sport takes place at the Oval?

3 Where was the 1990 soccer World Cup held?

4 What nationality is Severiano Ballesteros?

5 What sport is Steve Davis famous for?

6 Who performs in dressage?

7 What does LBW stand for?

8 How long is a marathon?

9 What track event has water jumps?

10 Who first ran a mile in under four minutes?

WHO WROTE THE CANTERBURY TALES?

The Canterbury Tales are the work of the English poet Geoffrey Chaucer (1342–1400).

The Canterbury Tales are a collection of stories in verse which are supposed to have been told by the different members of a party of 14th-century pilgrims on their way from London to Canterbury. The stories reflect the characters of the tellers, ranging from the bawdy miller's tale to the knight's story of honour and chivalry. Modern versions of the tales are still read today.

QUIZ 34

1 Who is Bjorn Borg?
2 In what event might a Fosbury flop be used?
3 Who won the 1991 Rugby World Cup?
4 Who won the 1990 soccer World Cup?
5 What event has a hop, step and jump?
6 What nationality is Carl Lewis?
7 What sport is Lucinda Green famous for?
8 What was Red Rum?
9 In what sport would you find a scrum-half?
10 What game is sometimes called ping-pong?

WHO WAS DON QUIXOTE?

Don Quixote was the hero of a 17th-century novel written by the author, Miguel de Cervantes (1547–1616).

Don Quixote is an eccentric old man who decides to become a knight and take on deeds of daring.
One of the best known stories in the book tells how because Don Quixote is short-sighted, he mistakes a row of windmills for giants, and sets about fighting them!

WHO MADE THE FIRST COLLECTIONS OF FAIRY TALES?

Many fairy tales are so old that we have no idea who first made them up – but we do know that the first collection of European traditional stories was made by the French writer, Charles Perrault, in 1697. Two collectors of fairy tales were the German brothers, Jacob Carl and Wilhelm Carl Grimm.

Perrault's stories included *Puss in Boots* and *Bluebeard*. Among the tales recorded by the Brothers Grimm were *Hansel and Gretel* and *Tom Thumb*.

WHO WAS ROBINSON CRUSOE?

Robinson Crusoe was the name of the hero of an adventure story about a ship-wrecked sailor. It was written by Daniel Defoe in 1719.

The story tells how Robinson Crusoe was cast up on a desert island, the only survivor of a shipwreck.

The idea of a poor castaway having to fend for himself on a desert island has always been popular. Defoe got the idea for the story from real-life tales of shipwrecked sailors – in particular the story of a man named Alexander Selkirk, very like Robinson Crusoe, who was well-known in Defoe's day.

QUIZ 35

1 Where did the game of golf originate?

2 For what sport are hands bandaged?

3 What sport was Pele famous for?

4 What country did Pele play for?

5 In bowls, what is the target ball called?

6 Who is the person who carries a golfer's clubs?

7 What bowling game is played on ice?

8 What is the New Zealand rugby team known as?

9 Which tribal group first played lacrosse?

10 How many people form a volleyball team?

WHO WROTE GULLIVER'S TRAVELS?

Gulliver's Travels is a satirical story about the adventures of a ship's doctor named Lemuel Gulliver. It was written by Jonathan Swift – a clergyman and scholar who lived from 1667 to 1745.

Swift was born in Ireland and educated in Trinity College Dublin. He eventually became Dean of St Patrick's Cathedral, Dublin. His writing is bitterly satirical and he was often very unpopular. Even *Gulliver's Travels*, though it is often told as an enjoyable story for children, was written he said, 'to vex the world'. It is in fact a disguised attack on the unpleasant aspects of life and politics in his own day.

QUIZ 36

1 Who throws the ball in baseball?

2 Where was basketball first played?

3 Is a softball pitched over- or underarm?

4 How many events are there in a heptathlon?

5 What is kept in a quiver?

6 What is a luge?

7 What indicates speed on squash balls?

8 What are cricket bats made from?

9 Where would you find a fairway and a bunker?

10 How long does a karate contest normally last?

WHO WAS EMILE ZOLA?

Emile Zola (1840–1902) was a French writer whose realistic (and often rather grim) novels set out to study life among ordinary people in the changing world of the Industrial Revolution.

Zola wrote a series of novels about two families, the Rougons and the Macquarts, and the problems of alcoholism. Other important novels in this series are Germinal, about a coal-mining community, and Nana, about a corrupt and beautiful young actress.

WHO CREATED FRANKENSTEIN'S MONSTER?

The story of the scientist Frankenstein, and the monster he made out of parts of other humans, was written by Mary Shelley (1797–1851).

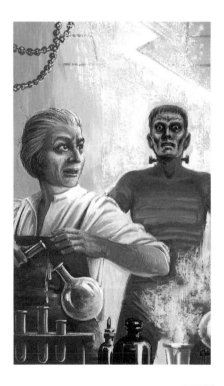

Mary Shelley was the wife of the famous poet Percy Bysshe Shelley.

Frankenstein tells how the monster made by Frankenstein saw so much cruelty and evil in the world that he turned against it. The story was published in 1818.

PEOPLE & PLACES

■ WHO WAS HONORÉ DE BALZAC?

Honoré de Balzac (1799–1850) was a French writer whose best known work is a series of about 100 novels and short stories to which he gave the overall title of **The Human Comedy.**

Balzac's novels, which are about provincial and Parisian life, include characters from many walks of life and cover themes such as fatherly love, greed and envy as well as dealing with many other aspects of life and politics in France.

■ WHO WAS VICTOR HUGO?

Victor Hugo (1802–1885) was a French poet, dramatist and novelist who is remembered today for two great novels – **The Hunchback of Notre Dame** *and* **Les Misérables.**

Victor Hugo was involved in politics which, in 1851, led to him having to live out of France for nearly 20 years. During this time he produced two books of poetry as well as his greatest novel, *Les Misérables*.

This tells the story of Jean Valjean, an escaped convict who tries to lead an honest and useful life. At the end of his life, Hugo returned to France. He died there in 1885.

QUIZ 37

1 In cricket, who stands behind the batsman?

2 In athletics, what is 'put' or thrown?

3 In athletics, what spear-like object is thrown?

4 In athletics, what field object is thrown by men only?

5 In athletics, what plate-like object is thrown?

6 What sports does the biathlon combine?

7 What sport has the 'snatch'?

8 What is a kayak?

9 What sport sometimes uses crossbows?

10 How many balls are used in pool?

WHO WERE THE THREE MUSKETEERS?

The Three Musketeers were the creations of the French writer Alexander Dumas (1803–1870). The musketeers, Porthos, Athos and Aramis, together with their friend d'Artagnan, were supposed to have been adventurers in 17th-century France.

Dumas also wrote the melodramatic *The Count of Monte Cristo* – the tale of a mysterious ex-prisoner bent on revenge for his unjust captivity.

WHO WAS HANS CHRISTIAN ANDERSEN?

Hans Christian Andersen (1805–1875) was Danish. He wrote children's stories, such as **The Ugly Duckling.**

QUIZ 38

1 What colour belt does a karate novice wear?

2 What is the highest colour karate belt?

3 What is the highest score with three darts?

4 What is fired to start a track event?

5 What is the referee called in tennis?

6 In what sport would you hit a puck?

7 What country hosts the baseball World Series?

8 What sport follows the Queensbury rules?

9 Did the explorer Marco Polo invent polo?

10 In soccer, what does a yellow card mean?

Hans Andersen's first book of stories had in it some of his best known – including *The Tinderbox* and *The Princess and the Pea* – but it was years before he was really successful. He based his stories on traditional tales, but many of them reflect his own rather sad and lonely life.

QUIZ 39

1 What are the Inuit people known as?

2 Where do the Inuit people live?

3 Who are the Romanies?

4 Who was Dame Margot Fonteyn?

5 What is W.G. Grace famous for?

6 What is Walter de la Mare famous for?

7 What is Florence Nightingale famous for?

8 What is Captain James Cook famous for?

9 What is Marcel Marceau famous for?

10 What is Joseph Haydn famous for?

■ WHO WAS MOBY DICK?

Moby Dick was a great white whale, whose story was written by the American, Herman Melville.

The story of Moby Dick is really the story of Captain Ahab, an old seafarer who spends his life trying to capture the great whale. Ahab has lost a leg in his hunt for Moby Dick, and finding him is an obsession. At the end of the story, Ahab's ship is lost and there is only one survivor.

■ WHO WROTE WAR AND PEACE?

War and Peace – often said to be one of the greatest novels ever written – was the work of the Russian writer Leo Tolstoy (1828–1910).

The book, set in the early 1800s, describes the lives of a group of aristocratic families and the effects on them of great historical events, such as Napoleon's attack on the city of Moscow. *Anna Karenina* is Tolstoy's other great novel. It tells of a woman who becomes an outcast from society.

WHO WAS CANDIDE?

Candide is the name of the hero of a satirical novel by the French writer Voltaire (1694–1778).

Candide tells the story of a young man who is convinced that we live in 'the best of all possible worlds'.

Voltaire attacked this optimism by describing how Candide, after being involved in many horrific adventures, eventually comes to the conclusion that the best we can do is go and 'cultivate our own gardens'.

QUIZ 40

1 Who was Sir Christopher Wren?

2 Who was Van Dyck?

3 What were conquistadors?

4 Who was Stanley Matthews?

5 Where does Mother Theresa care for the poor?

6 What were peelers in the nineteenth century?

7 What is Sir John Gielgud famous for?

8 Who was Sir John Betjeman?

9 What is Jane Austen famous for?

10 What is Babe Ruth famous for?

WHO WAS FRANZ KAFKA?

Franz Kafka (1883–1924) was a writer in German, though he was born in Czechoslovakia and spent most of his life there. His best known works are two novels – The Castle and The Trial, and a short story, Metamorphosis.

Kafka was an anxious and lonely man, and this is reflected in his books, which are often about people who seem to suffer in a cold and unsympathetic world for no clear reason. He has influenced many 20th century writers.

DID SHERLOCK HOLMES EXIST?

Sherlock Holmes must be one of the most famous detectives of all time – but the truth is that he was not a real person at all. He was the creation of the novelist Sir Arthur Conan Doyle (1859–1930).

Sherlock Holmes was not the first fictional detective (Edgar Allen Poe had already created M. Dupin). But he was the first to catch the public imagination, and his character and lifestyle were so well described that many people have believed he was real and have looked for his house.

QUIZ 41

1 Which country is the island of Sulawesi in?

2 Which country was once known as Cathay?

3 Which island is known in its own language as Kalaallit Nunaat?

4 What is Iceland's main export?

5 Where is the Royal Pavilion?

6 What country did King Zog rule?

7 What do aborigines call Uluru?

8 What country do Flemings live in?

9 What city was once called New Amsterdam?

10 Which country do the Hindu Kush Mountains cross?

WHO MADE THE GUITAR A CONCERT INSTRUMENT?

The guitar is a traditional instrument which until the 20th century was used mainly to play the folk music of Spain. Today it is a concert instrument as well – a development that is almost entirely the result of the work of the guitarist Andres Segovia.

Segovia was born in Spain in 1894. He became interested in the idea of arranging classical music for the guitar. He began with lute music, and then went on to make arrangements of music by many composers, including JS Bach and Handel.

PEOPLE & PLACES

WHO WAS ELVIS PRESLEY?

Elvis Presley was one of the first 'pop' stars – a rock 'n' roll singer whose appearance on stage could almost cause a riot. He was most popular in the 1950s and 1960s with songs such as Heartbreak Hotel *and* Jailhouse Rock.

Born in 1935, Elvis came from a poor family from the deep south of America. In 1955 he was signed on by a big record company. Soon he was an international star – though not popular with everyone. He wore bright clothes, sang loudly with a strong rhythm and wiggled his hips as he sang. Many people were shocked!

QUIZ 42

1 Which range of hills is Cheddar Gorge in?

2 Which continent does the River Orinoco flow through?

3 Where is Mount Bruce?

4 Which country has a town called Batman?

5 Which is the largest state in the USA?

6 Which country is Corsica a part of?

7 What is the national emblem of China?

8 Which country is covered by the Kalahari Desert?

9 What is the main crop of Sri Lanka?

10 Where are the Cascade Mountains?

WHO WERE THE BEATLES?

The Beatles were a group of four rock musicians from Liverpool who became famous in the 1960s.

The four Beatles were John Lennon (1940–1980), Paul McCartney (born 1942), George Harrison (born 1943) and Ringo Starr (whose real name was Richard Starkey – born 1940). The group's early years were spent largely in Hamburg and in Liverpool. Success came in 1962, with a song called *Love Me Do*. The Beatles soon became the most successful group in the history of pop music. After making several albums, The Beatles broke up in 1970.

45

PEOPLE & PLACES

WHERE WERE IRON WEAPONS FIRST USED IN WAR?

War in ancient times was fought at close range. The first soldiers to use iron weapons were the Assyrians.

QUIZ 43

1 Which country once had a ruler called Montezuma?
2 Which country is Legoland in?
3 Where is Midway Island?
4 Where is Olduvai Gorge?
5 Which country was once known as Hibernia?
6 Which country sold Florida to the USA?
7 Which modern city was once known as Byzantium and Constantinople?
8 Where is the Golden Temple?
9 Which state of the USA is Disneyland in?
10 Which country are the Aleutian Islands part of?

The first real armies were those of Assyria and Egypt, some 3000 years ago. Egypt had many soldiers but few wore any kind of protective clothing. Egyptian archers used reed arrows tipped with stone or copper.

Iron, the new metal, was harder and sharper. The Assyrians discovered how to use it in warfare. They made iron heads for their spears and arrows. For defence, the Assyrian soldiers wore long coats of iron chain-mail.

WHO INVENTED THE ROCKET?

The Chinese invented the rocket by packing tubes with gunpowder. From this simple firework have come today's space rockets.

The Chinese discovered thousands of years ago that gunpowder explodes when burned. Packed into a tube, the exploding gunpowder pushes out a stream of hot gas, sending the tube flying off in the opposite direction.
The Chinese let off fireworks for fun, but also fired rockets as weapons of war.

WHAT ARE GUERRILLAS?

Guerrillas are fighters who make hit-and-run raids on enemy forces during a war. They tend to fight in small groups, not as part of a main army, and might not wear uniforms. The word guerrilla is Spanish for 'little war'.

Bands of guerrillas often fight behind enemy lines. They make sudden attacks against enemy outposts, ambush convoys of enemy lorries, or blow up enemy trains. Guerrillas often find food and hiding places with help from people who live in the area. They usually shelter in places where they can hide from attack easily.

By choosing when and where to attack, a small band of guerrillas can make trouble for a far larger enemy force.

QUIZ 44

1 Which country has the lotus flower as its national emblem?
2 Which country has the hibiscus as its national emblem?
3 What is the emblem of Berne?
4 What religion do most Burmese people belong to?
5 What is the main language in the island of Haiti?
6 Which country has the most pigs in the world?
7 Which city has more canals, Birmingham or Venice?
8 Which country's flag shows an eagle, a snake and a cactus?
9 What is a maelstrom?
10 Which sea is to the north of Turkey?

WHAT ARE MERCENARIES?

Mercenaries are soldiers prepared to fight in any war for any side that pays them. The word mercenary comes from a Latin word meaning 'wages'. Some fight just for money, others more for adventure.

The most famous mercenary fighting unit has long been France's Foreign Legion. It was formed in 1831. It takes anyone from any country if they are young and fit enough to fight.

PEOPLE & PLACES

■ WHERE WERE THE FIRST OLYMPIC GAMES HELD?

Every four years, from 776 BC, the Greeks held a great festival. Artists, writers and athletes gathered to honour the great god Zeus. The contests were held

at Olympia, and became known as the Olympic Games.

The first Olympic Games were not just sporting contests. There were plays and recitals by poets, as well as races. To the Greeks, the Games expressed the union of mind and body, striving for victory to honour Zeus, the king of the gods.

The events lasted for three days. Athletes ran, wrestled, rode horses and drove chariots. The Games began with the Olympic oath and ended with prizes and feasting.

■ WHY ARE VERY LONG RACES KNOWN AS MARATHON EVENTS?

The highlight of long-distance racing in the Olympics is the marathon. It takes its name from a legendary run made by a Greek soldier in 490 BC.

The soldier raced from the plain of Marathon to Athens to announce the news of a great victory over an army of Persians.

QUIZ 45

1 What drink would a Russian make in a samovar?

2 Which country do frankfurters come from?

3 Which man-made structure can be seen from the Moon?

4 Where does pasta come from?

5 Where do gouda and edam cheeses come from?

6 Which islands are famous for their giant tortoises?

7 To which country do the Galapagos Islands belong?

8 Which mountain range do llamas live in?

9 Where did the Inca people live?

10 What is Shinto?

WHY DO RUNNERS USE STARTING BLOCKS?

Starting blocks allow a sprinter to drive forward smoothly and powerfully, and to reach top speed much more quickly than if a standing start was used. The blocks are only needed in sprint races.

Until 1884, sprinters started in standing or leaning positions. That year, a runner began to use a crouched position with one foot in front of the other, and both hands touching the ground. From this coiled crouch a runner could spring forward at full racing speed.

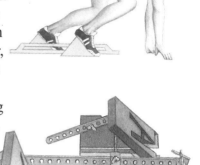

WHY DO RUNNERS START FROM DIFFERENT POSITIONS IN SOME TRACK RACES?

When track races are run in lanes, the runners on the outside cover more distance than those on the inside as they come round bends. To ensure that everyone travels the same distance, the runners start at staggered intervals.

It is in the 200-metre and 400-metre sprints, in which all the runners travel flat out in different lanes, that staggered starting positions are needed.

QUIZ 46

1 Where is Mount Ararat?

2 What crop is grown in paddy fields?

3 Where are the Appalachian Mountains?

4 Where is Mount St Helens?

5 Which sea does the Nile flow into?

6 Where are the tea-producing areas of Assam and Darjeeling?

7 Which is the largest lake in Africa?

8 What valuable product is Texas famous for?

9 Where does Count Dracula come from?

10 Where is Transylvania?

WHY ARE POLE-VAULTERS NOT HURT WHEN THEY LAND?

A fall from a height of more than 5 metres (16 feet) on to one's back or shoulders could break bones. To avoid this, pole-vaulters land in special pits filled with soft inflated airbags.

Pole-vaulters make a long approach-run to the hurdle to build up speed. As they approach the uprights, they plant one end of the lightweight fibreglass pole in a sunken take-off box. In a single continuous motion they hurl themselves upwards, swinging feet first towards the bar. As the vaulters continue to pull their feet upward, the right leg crosses over the left leg. The chest is now next to the cross-bar. At the last moment they push the pole away and twist over the cross-bar.

QUIZ 47

1 Which is the longest river in Europe?
2 Which is the least crowded country in the world?
3 Which country's flag has a maple leaf on it?
4 Which country's flag is a plain green rectangle?
5 Which European country is famous for fjords?
6 Which country is famous as the home of the kiwi?
7 Where do the Maori people come from?
8 What is an oasis?
9 Where is the Great Rift Valley?
10 Where is the Dead Sea?

WHY IS GYMNASTICS AN OLYMPIC SPORT?

Gymnastics was a highly popular activity in ancient Greece. Interest in the sport was revived in the 19th century and it was included in the first modern Olympics in 1896. Women's gymnastics was restricted to only one event until 1952.

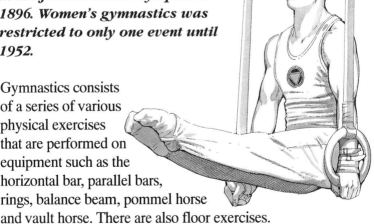

Gymnastics consists of a series of various physical exercises that are performed on equipment such as the horizontal bar, parallel bars, rings, balance beam, pommel horse and vault horse. There are also floor exercises.

WHY DO MOST GOLFERS HAVE HANDICAPS?

A handicap is a way of scoring so that a good player can be fairly matched with a weaker player. Each golfer is given minus points, depending on the average number of strokes he or she needs to complete the game. Better golfers take fewer strokes so they have lower handicaps. Weak golfers have higher handicaps because they take more strokes.

The aim of golf is for each player to hit the ball from the starting point, or tee, into a small hole with the least number of strokes. The golfer uses a selection of different clubs. The distance between the tee and the hole can be from 90–550 metres (100 to 600 yards). A complete game has 18 holes.

QUIZ 48

1 Which sea is Cyprus in?
2 Where would you find the island called Muckle Flugga?
3 Is The Wash wet?
4 Which sea are Jamaica and Cuba in?
5 Which sea is the island of Gotland in?
6 Where is the island of Hokkaido?
7 Where was the first atomic bomb dropped?
8 Which country is the Suez Canal in?
9 Which country does Tasmania belong to?
10 Which is the world's largest ocean?

WHY IS REAL TENNIS DIFFERENT FROM TENNIS?

Real tennis, or royal tennis, was first played in the Middle Ages. It is played on an indoor court divided in two by a net. The ball may be hit against the sloping roof of the court.

The game of modern tennis, or lawn tennis, was devised in England in 1873. This game is played on level grass courts or hard-surface courts.

PEOPLE & PLACES

WHAT IS A PENTATHLON?

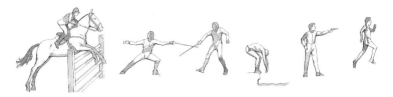

A pentathlon is a five-part competition for athletes. Its name comes from the Greek words pente, meaning five, and athlon, meaning contest. In a pentathlon each contestant must take part in five different events. The winner is the one with the highest score.

In ancient Greece and Rome the chosen events were ones thought to test all the strengths and skills of an athlete. The modern pentathlon tests riding, fencing, swimming, shooting and running 4000 metres.

QUIZ 49

1 How much of the Earth is covered by water?

2 What is the deepest trench in the world?

3 Which ocean is it in?

4 What is the largest sea in the world?

5 Where is the world's largest bay?

6 Which ocean is it part of?

7 Which ocean is the island of Madagascar in?

8 Apart from Australia, which is the largest island in the world?

9 Where is the world's tallest waterfall?

10 Which is the world's smallest country?

WHY DO ROWING TEAMS OFTEN CARRY PASSENGERS?

Rowing teams of four and eight people are often steered by a coxswain, who does not row. He or she has the important job of steering the boat and setting the pace of the strokes made by the rowers.

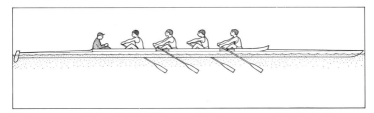

The rowers sit in single file on sliding seats with their feet braced against stretchers. Each person uses a single oar. These are set on alternate sides of the boat.

WHY ARE SOME STYLES OF SWIMMING FASTER THAN OTHERS?

Water forms a barrier to the human body as it tries to move through it. Some styles of swimming reduce resistance to the water more than others. This makes them faster.

The most efficient, and therefore the fastest, way of travelling through water is a stroke called the crawl. With this stroke, the body cuts through the shallowest amount of water.

Other major styles of swimming include the backstroke, the butterfly stroke and the breast stroke.

WHY DO SURFBOARDS TRAVEL SO SWIFTLY?

Surfboards skim the surface at speeds much faster than the water may be moving.

Surfers control their speed and direction by shifting the weight of their bodies back and forward along the board. Surfing first became a popular sport in Hawaii, Australia and the west coast of America, where the long Pacific swells made the wave conditions ideal.

QUIZ 50

1 Where is the world's deepest cave?

2 Where is the world's longest cave?

3 Which is the longest river in Britain?

4 Which is the largest lake in the United Kingdom?

5 Which is the longest river in the British Isles?

6 Which river has the world's largest delta?

7 Which river has the greatest flow of water in the world?

8 Where are the world's tallest sand dunes?

9 Where is the world's longest mountain range?

10 Which is the highest mountain in the world?

WHEN DID THE MARTIAL ARTS FIRST DEVELOP?

The martial arts are methods of self-defence and combat. They began in Japan and evolved into sports at the end of the 19th century and beginning of the 20th century. They are based on techniques which are centuries old, such as those of jujitsu.

Typical martial arts are judo, karate, aikido, sumo and kendo. Only kendo involves the use of weapons. The others involve methods of hitting, kicking, throwing, choking or holding an opponent.

Judo

Kendo

Karate

WHY ARE COLOURED BELTS WORN IN KARATE?

A karate fighter's level of skill is shown by the colour of the belt he or she wears. Masters wear black belts. Students wear brown, blue, green and orange belts, down to white belts for beginners. Students move from one grade to the next by taking exams.

Karate fighters train to focus the entire muscle power of their body into one blow of great force. Hands, fists, elbows and feet are all used to deliver karate blows.

QUIZ 51

1 Which is the world's largest saltwater lake?

2 Which is the world's largest freshwater lake?

3 Which is the world's largest desert?

4 Which ocean does the Amazon flow into?

5 Which gulf does the Mississippi flow into?

6 Which ocean does the Zaire river flow into?

7 Which country has the most borders with other countries?

8 Which is the world's largest city?

9 Which is the oldest temple in the world?

10 Where is Angkor Wat?

WHY ARE SUMO WRESTLERS GIANTS?

Sumo wrestlers are enormous men. The best fighters stand well over 1.83 metres high and may weigh 130 kilograms or more. The bigger a wrestler is, the greater are his chances of becoming a champion.

Sumo wrestling takes place in a small sand ring. The object of the fight is for one wrestler either to down his opponent by forcing him to the ground or to drive him physically out of the ring.

QUIZ 52

1 Which is the largest church in the world?

2 Where is the world's largest Buddhist temple?

3 Where is the world's largest Mormon temple?

4 Where is the world's largest mosque?

5 Where is the world's deepest gold mine?

6 Where is the world's deepest water well?

7 Where is the world's longest glacier?

8 Which country has the most volcanoes?

9 Which is the world's largest volcano?

10 Which continent has the hottest temperatures?

WHY IS SOCCER SO POPULAR?

Soccer is the world's most popular sport, and is played in every continent in the world.

The rules of soccer were laid down in Britain in the 1860s when the Football Association was formed to control the sport. It is really a simple game in which two teams of 11 players try to score by kicking a ball into the opposing team's goal-mouth.

Players control the ball with their feet or head, but they are not allowed to touch it with their arms and hands. Only the goalkeeper may handle the ball, and then only inside the penalty area in front of his own goal-mouth.

QUIZ 53

1 Where do the Kalash people live?
2 Where do the Tuareg people live?
3 What is the capital of Nepal?
4 What is the capital of Mongolia?
5 What is a Muslim holy man called?
6 What is a Jewish holy man called?
7 Has anyone ever found a Yeti?
8 In which continent were the oldest human remains found?
9 Where are the Everglades?
10 Where is the Okavango?

WHAT IS THE FASTEST BALL GAME?

This is one of several games played with a small, hard ball known as a pelota *(the Spanish for ball). The fastest pelota game is* jai alai. *It is played in the Basque region, but may have begun in 13th-century Italy.*

The players wear a long, basket-like *cesta* strapped to one arm. They use the cesta to catch and throw the small, hard rubber ball.

WHEN WAS BASKETBALL FIRST PLAYED?

Basketball was played for the first time in December 1891, in America. It was devised to inspire students who were bored with their physical education class.

The first goals were two peach baskets. The iron hoop and net was introduced two years later. People had to climb a ladder to get the ball from the net. Cutting a hole in the net so that the ball could drop through came later.

Today, basketball is a popular sport all over the world.

WHEN WERE THE FIRST MOTOR RACES?

The first motor race was in 1895 in France. It ran from Paris to Bordeaux and back. The winner was Emile Levassor, who did more than 48 hours driving at an average speed of 24 kilometres an hour.

The Grand Prix series of races was begun in 1906 by French car makers. These still take place every year.

WHAT IS FORMULA ONE MOTOR RACING?

This is the world's top rank type of motor racing. All the most important of the Grand Prix races are those between Formula One racing cars.

A Formula One racing car is low and wedge-shaped. Such cars can reach 320 kilometres an hour. The races are about 320 kilometres long. They are run on circuits with straight, fast stretches, and sharp bends.

QUIZ 54

1 Where is the Hunza Valley?

2 Which city has the nickname ''Frisco''?

3 Which island produces most of the world's cloves?

4 Where is the town of Mandalay?

5 What animal appears on Australia's coat-of-arms?

6 Which country produces most of the world's dates?

7 What was Covent Garden famous for?

8 Which Italian city is the home of the Leaning Tower?

9 Which way would the ruins point if the Leaning Tower fell down?

10 Where is the Irrawaddy?

PEOPLE & PLACES

■ WHY ARE SKIS SO LONG?

Long skis give a skier more control than short ones. On a steep slope, most of the ski simply slides over the surface. It is the edge of the ski which bites into the snow and allows a skier to change direction and speed. The greater the surface of ski that is in contact with the ground, the more it control it offers to the skier.

Cross-country skis are used for travelling on flat slopes, rather than downhill. They are very narrow.

■ WHAT IS FIGURE SKATING?

This is one of the main ice-skating sports. (Two others are speed skating and ice dancing.) Figure skating involves skating patterns called figures on ice.

Figure-skating contests have two main parts – school figures and free skating. School figures are based on a figure-of-eight pattern, and may be skated on both skates or only one. They include about 70 variations. Free skating is freer than schools skating. In pairs skating, a man and woman skate together.

QUIZ 55

1 What continent is Lake Chad in?

2 What continent are the Great Lakes in?

3 What continent is Lake Titicaca in?

4 Which Scottish loch is said to contain a monster?

5 What continent is the Atacama Desert in?

6 Which two countries does the Gobi Desert cross?

7 Which Wall was pulled down in 1990?

8 Which is the smallest country in South America?

9 Which island is the world's largest coral atoll?

10 What religion do most Indonesians belong to?

QUIZ 56

1 Where are cows considered to be sacred?

2 Which country is nearest to the Coral Sea?

3 In which two countries do Navajo indians now live?

4 Which country is Timbuktu in?

5 What crop is Cuba's main export?

6 Which country has a cherry blossom festival?

7 What are people from the Orkney Islands called?

8 Where are the Karakoram Mountains?

9 Which country sold Alaska to the USA?

10 Which sea is most polluted by oil?

WHERE DO ABORIGINES LIVE?

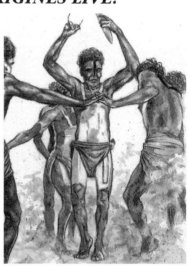

Aborigines are a country's earliest inhabitants. The best known are those of Australia.

There were about 300,000 Aborigines in Australia when Europeans first arrived there. Now only about 110,000 remain. Australian Aborigines have their own music, art and religion. At times they gather for a corroboree, a festival of music and dancing. One of their weapons is the boomerang, a wooden throwing weapon. The lighter kind of boomerang is cleverly designed to return to the thrower.

WHERE DO MAORIS LIVE?

The Maoris are the native people of New Zealand. Indeed the word Maori *means 'native'.*

Maoris speak a Polynesian language. Hundreds of years ago, their ancestors sailed from far-off Pacific islands in huge canoes. They were the first people to settle in New Zealand. They were skilled carvers, tattooists and weavers.

PEOPLE & PLACES

◾ WHERE DO THE TUAREG LIVE?

The Tuareg are nomads of northern Africa. Some roam the Sahara Desert. Others live and trade across its southern edge.

The Tuareg belong to the Berber peoples, who lived in North Africa long before the Arabs arrived. They speak the old Tuareg language and use an ancient kind of writing. The Tuareg are Muslims. In contrast to many Muslims, the Tuareg men, not the women, veil their faces. There are two Tuareg classes: nobles and vassals. Nobles own camels, goats, sheep and farms set in oases. Vassals mind the nobles' livestock.

◾ WHERE DO PYGMIES LIVE?

Pygmies are very small people, mostly living a primitive life. Groups live in remote parts of Africa, the Andaman Islands of the Indian Ocean, Malaysia and the Philippines. Their numbers are few and becoming fewer still.

The best known pygmies are the Negrillos, who live in Central Africa. A full grown Negrillo is no taller than a ten-year-old boy of normal height.

QUIZ 57

1 Can you sneeze with your eyes open?

2 What was the Bastille?

3 Which US state is the town of Kermit in?

4 Where is Zagazig?

5 How many centimes in one French franc?

6 What did Christopher Sholes invent?

7 When was the ball point pen invented?

8 How many centimetres are there in a kilometre?

9 What colour does acid turn litmus paper?

10 Where is Ouagadougou?

▪ *WHERE DO ESKIMOS LIVE?*

Eskimos live in the cold polar regions of North America and north-east Asia. They are related to the Chinese and Japanese. Their ancestors probably migrated across the Arctic.

Eskimos have learnt how to cope with the cold. They make warm fur coats and build turf-roofed homes, half hidden underground. In winter, hunters far out on the ice build snow houses called igloos. But many Eskimos now live in wooden houses in towns.

▪ *WHERE DO LAPPS LIVE?*

Lapps live mostly in a region of the Arctic called Lapland which covers parts of northern Europe.

The Lapps' ancestors lived in Central Asia. Lapps have their own language. They wear colourful clothes of wool and reindeer skins. Mountain Lapps lead a wandering life with their reindeer herds. River Lapps live a more settled life along river banks. Sea Lapps live in wood huts built on the coast and work as fishermen.

QUIZ 58

1 What is a double top in darts?

2 When was the longest game of baseball played?

3 Who was it between?

4 When was the soccer World Cup first played?

5 Where is the largest sports stadium in the world?

6 How long is a game of Australian football?

7 Which is the fastest of all ball games?

8 Whose long jump record was unbroken for 25 years?

9 Who was Red Rum?

10 In Karate, what does 'Hajime!' mean?

PEOPLE & PLACES

QUIZ 1
1. A dance
2. Isadora Duncan
3. Spain
4. Ballerinas
5. Tchaikovsky
6. The Nutcracker
7. Fred Astaire
8. A choreographer
9. Two
10. Sleeping Beauty

QUIZ 2
1. Soprano
2. Bass
3. Tenor
4. Sing
5. None
6. A brass instrument
7. Saxophone
8. Double bass
9. Four
10. Mozart

QUIZ 3
1. Beethoven
2. Flute
3. Violin
4. The lyrics
5. Gustav Holst
6. Edward Elgar
7. Play slowly
8. South America
9. Trumpet
10. Lyre

QUIZ 4
1. The harp
2. Russia
3. Drums
4. A guitar
5. Wolfgang Amadeus
6. A composer
7. Beethoven
8. Vivaldi
9. Chopin
10. Operas

QUIZ 5
1. Violins
2. W.S.Gilbert
3. Japan
4. German
5. The Royal Albert Hall
6. A baton
7. Woodwind
8. J.S. Bach
9. Electric instruments
10. India

QUIZ 6
1. Van Gogh
2. Toulouse Lautrec
3. Michelangelo
4. Spanish
5. Pablo Picasso
6. Leonardo da Vinci
7. The Louvre
8. Italian
9. Venus de Milo
10. Constable

QUIZ 7
1. A watercolour
2. French
3. Easels
4. Studios
5. A sculptor
6. Van Gogh
7. French
8. English
9. Landscapes
10. Portraits

QUIZ 8
1. Plays
2. Stratford-upon-Avon
3. Anne Hathaway
4. London
5. Juliet
6. Irish
7. A pantomime
8. Aladdin
9. 19th century
10. Shakespeare

QUIZ 9

1. *Denmark*
2. *Richard III*
3. *Cleopatra*
4. *Desdemona*
5. *Shylock*
6. *An actor*
7. *Bottom*
8. *A sprite*
9. Romeo and Juliet
10. Peter Pan

QUIZ 10

1. *A cinema*
2. The Jazz Singer
3. *A comedian*
4. *Westerns*
5. *Marilyn Monroe*
6. *Los Angeles*
7. *Julie Andrews*
8. *Mickey Mouse*
9. The Temple of Doom
10. *Harrison Ford*

QUIZ 11

1. *The Joker*
2. *Robin*
3. *A film award*
4. The Wizard of Oz
5. *Talkies*
6. *James Bond*
7. *Ian Fleming*
8. *Q*
9. *Stan and Oliver*
10. *The* Star Wars *series*

QUIZ 12

1. SS Enterprise
2. *Captain Kirk*
3. *A car*
4. *The Lone Ranger*
5. *Cartoons*
6. *Donald Duck*
7. *Tom and Jerry*
8. *Humphrey Bogart*
9. Gone with the Wind
10. *Marlon Brando*

QUIZ 13

1. *Puppets*
2. *Judy*
3. *Magicians*
4. *A clown*
5. *The ringmaster*
6. *Tightrope walking*
7. *A dummy*
8. *Chess*
9. *52*
10. *A bullfighter*

QUIZ 14

1. *Islam*
2. *Judaism*
3. *Buddhism*
4. *Judaism*
5. *The Pope*
6. *Tibet*
7. *The Mormons*
8. *Genesis*
9. *Revelations*
10. *Submission*

QUIZ 15

1. *A language*
2. *Gutenberg*
3. *An atlas*
4. *Fables*
5. *The hare*
6. *A poem*
7. *Robert Burns*
8. *William*
9. *Nature*
10. *The Lake District*

QUIZ 16

1. *Irish*
2. *Hiawatha*
3. *Ted Hughes*
4. *T.S. Eliot*
5. Cats
6. *Westminster Abbey*
7. *Japan*
8. *The albatross*
9. *Edward Lear*
10. *The Dong*

PEOPLE & PLACES

QUIZ 17
1. Louisa May Alcott
2. Female
3. No
4. Dr Watson
5. 221B Baker Street
6. Moriarty
7. The Three Musketeers
8. Robinson Crusoe
9. A hobbit
10. Gandalf

QUIZ 18
1. The Brontës
2. Wuthering Heights
3. Rip Van Winkle
4. Gulliver
5. Mark Twain
6. C.S. Lewis
7. Aslan
8. J.M. Barrie
9. Tinker Bell
10. Captain Hook

QUIZ 19
1. Charles Dickens
2. Pickwick Papers
3. A Christmas Carol
4. Three
5. Oliver Twist
6. Charles Kingsley
7. The Robinsons
8. Jim Hawkins
9. Long John Silver
10. Robert Louis Stevenson

QUIZ 20
1. In prison
2. Phineas Fogg
3. Passepartout
4. Jane Eyre
5. Tom Brown
6. Rugby School
7. Tom
8. Anne
9. Rebecca
10. Historical romances

QUIZ 21
1. A scarecrow
2. Mowgli
3. Baloo
4. Winnie-the-Pooh
5. A donkey
6. Roald Dahl
7. Willie Wonka
8. Wonderland
9. Tweedledum
10. Enid Blyton

QUIZ 22
1. Toad
2. Wind in the Willows
3. Poems and novels
4. 40
5. Detective novels
6. Belgian
7. Miss Marple
8. The Orient Express
9. Hamelin
10. A sailor

QUIZ 23
1. Lord of the Flies
2. The Dump
3. Animals
4. Arthur Ransome
5. It was secret
6. Anna Sewell
7. Greyfriars
8. Eating
9. Beatrix Potter
10. A hedgehog

QUIZ 24
1. Languages
2. Barrels
3. A blacksmith!
4. Nuns
5. Very Important Person
6. Dictionaries
7. Postage stamps
8. Women's hats
9. Church bells
10. Wood

QUIZ 25
1. The dollar
2. The franc
3. The rouble
4. The guilder
5. The peso
6. Japan
7. Germany
8. Spain
9. Italy
10. India

QUIZ 26
1. Mexico
2. Switzerland
3. Holland
4. India
5. Ireland
6. Wales
7. Spain
8. Australia
9. Scotland
10. Japan

QUIZ 27
1. Guatemala City
2. Australia
3. Buenos Aires
4. The Seine
5. The Ganges
6. Reykjavik
7. Ireland
8. Venice
9. Tegucigalpa
10. Blarney stone

QUIZ 28
1. Brussels
2. The Thames
3. Tanzania
4. Wellington
5. Venezuela
6. The Indian Ocean
7. The Stars and Stripes
8. The Union Jack
9. The Southern Cross
10. The Tricolore

QUIZ 29
1. Ten
2. Every four years
3. Basketball
4. Darts and archery
5. 11
6. Ice dancing
7. Badminton
8. Boxing
9. American football
10. Motorcycle racing

QUIZ 30
1. Golf
2. Horse racing
3. Cyclists
4. A yellow jersey
5. Seven
6. Track
7. Dragsters (cars)
8. On a green
9. Yacht racing
10. Fencing

QUIZ 31
1. American football
2. Baseball
3. 13
4. A martial art
5. Japan
6. The black
7. Billiards and pool
8. A jockey
9. A wicket
10. Tennis

QUIZ 32
1. The relay
2. Light-flyweight
3. Gymnastics
4. Bobsleigh
5. Australia and England
6. 11
7. A stroke in swimming
8. Barcelona, Spain
9. Albertville, France
10. Polo

PEOPLE & PLACES

QUIZ 33
1. Motor racing
2. Cricket
3. Italy
4. Spanish
5. Snooker
6. A horse and rider
7. Leg before wicket
8. 42.2 kilometres
9. The steeplechase
10. Roger Bannister

QUIZ 34
1. A tennis player
2. The high jump
3. Australia
4. Germany
5. The triple jump
6. American
7. Three-day eventing
8. A horse
9. Rugby
10. Table tennis

QUIZ 35
1. Scotland
2. Boxing
3. Soccer
4. Brazil
5. The jack
6. The caddie
7. Curling
8. The All Blacks
9. American Indians
10. Six

QUIZ 36
1. The pitcher
2. USA
3. Underarm
4. Seven
5. Arrows
6. A one-person toboggan
7. Coloured spots
8. Willow
9. A golf course
10. Two minutes

QUIZ 37
1. The wicketkeeper
2. The shot
3. The javelin
4. The hammer
5. The discus
6. Skiing and shooting
7. Weight-lifting
8. A canoe
9. Archery
10. 16

QUIZ 38
1. White
2. Black
3. 180
4. A pistol
5. The umpire
6. Ice hockey
7. USA
8. Boxing
9. No
10. A warning

QUIZ 39
1. Eskimos
2. The Arctic
3. Gypsies
4. A ballerina
5. Cricket
6. Poetry
7. Nursing
8. Sailing to Australia
9. Mime
10. Composing

QUIZ 40
1. An architect
2. A painter
3. Spanish explorers
4. A footballer
5. India
6. Policemen
7. Acting
8. A poet
9. Writing novels
10. Playing baseball

PEOPLE & PLACES

QUIZ 41
1. Indonesia
2. China
3. Greenland
4. Fish
5. Brighton, UK
6. Albania
7. Ayers Rock
8. Belgium
9. New York (Manhattan)
10. Afghanistan

QUIZ 42
1. Mendips
2. South America
3. Australia
4. Turkey
5. Alaska
6. France
7. A dragon
8. Botswana
9. Tea
10. Washington State, USA

QUIZ 43
1. Mexico
2. Denmark
3. The Pacific
4. Tanzania
5. Ireland
6. Spain
7. Istanbul
8. Amritsar, India
9. California
10. USA

QUIZ 44
1. India
2. Malaysia
3. A bear
4. Buddhism
5. French
6. China
7. Birmingham
8. Mexico's
9. A whirlpool
10. The Black Sea

QUIZ 45
1. Tea
2. Germany
3. Great Wall of China
4. Italy
5. The Netherlands
6. The Galapagos
7. Ecuador
8. The Andes
9. Peru
10. A Japanese religion

QUIZ 46
1. Turkey
2. Rice
3. USA
4. Washington State, USA
5. The Mediterranean
6. India
7. Lake Victoria
8. Oil
9. Transylvania
10. Romania

QUIZ 47
1. The Volga
2. Mongolia
3. Canada
4. Libya's
5. Norway
6. New Zealand
7. New Zealand
8. A water hole
9. Africa
10. Israel/Jordan

QUIZ 48
1. Mediterranean
2. The Shetlands, Scotland
3. Yes
4. The Caribbean
5. The Baltic
6. Japan
7. Hiroshima, Japan
8. Egypt
9. Australia
10. The Pacific

PEOPLE & PLACES

QUIZ 49
1. 70%
2. Marianas Trench
3. The Pacific
4. South China Sea
5. The Bay of Bengal
6. Indian Ocean
7. Indian Ocean
8. Greenland
9. Angel Falls, Venezuela
10. Vatican City

QUIZ 50
1. France
2. Kentucky, USA
3. The Severn
4. Lough Neagh
5. The Shannon
6. The Ganges
7. The Amazon
8. The Sahara
9. Under the Atlantic
10. Mount Everest

QUIZ 51
1. Caspian Sea
2. Lake Superior
3. Sahara
4. Atlantic
5. Gulf of Mexico
6. Atlantic
7. China
8. Tokyo
9. Angkor Wat
10. Cambodia

QUIZ 52
1. St Peter's, Rome
2. Borobudur, Indonesia
3. Salt Lake Temple, USA
4. Islamabad, Pakistan
5. South Africa
6. Montana, USA
7. Antarctica
8. Indonesia
9. Mauna Loa, Hawaii
10. Africa

QUIZ 53
1. Northern Pakistan
2. Sahara desert
3. Kathmandu
4. Ulan Batur
5. An imam
6. A rabbi
7. No
8. Africa
9. Florida, USA
10. Botswana, Africa

QUIZ 54
1. Northern Pakistan
2. San Francisco
3. Zanzibar
4. Myanmar (Burma)
5. Kangaroo
6. Iraq
7. Its fruit market
8. Pisa
9. South
10. Burma

QUIZ 55
1. Africa
2. North America
3. South America
4. Loch Ness
5. South America
6. China and Mongolia
7. The Berlin Wall
8. Uruguay
9. Kwajalein
10. Islam

QUIZ 56
1. India
2. Australia
3. USA and Canada
4. Mali
5. Sugar
6. Japan
7. Orcadians
8. Central Asia
9. Russia
10. The Mediterranean

PEOPLE & PLACES

QUIZ 57

1. No
2. A prison
3. Texas
4. Egypt
5. 100
6. The typewriter
7. 1938
8. 100,000
9. Red
10. Burkina Faso

QUIZ 58

1. A score of double 20
2. In 1920
3. Boston and Brooklyn
4. In 1930
5. Prague, Czechoslovakia
6. 100 mins
7. Pelota
8. Jesse Owens
9. A racehorse
10. 'Begin!' (a contest)

INDEX